A HANDBOOK FOR BUSY PARENTS

Cause Children Don't Come with Instructions

Elder Thomas "Uncle Thomas" Colbert, III

ISBN 978-1-0980-6679-6 (paperback)
ISBN 978-1-0980-6680-2 (hardcover)
ISBN 978-1-0980-6681-9 (digital)

Christian Faith Publishing, Inc.
832 Park Avenue
Meadville, PA 16335
www.christianfaithpublishing.com

All scriptures are from the King James Version of the Bible unless otherwise indicated.

Scriptures marked (NIV) are taken from the NEW INTERNATIONAL VERSION (NIV): Scripture taken from THE HOLY BIBLE, NEW INTERNATIONAL VERSION®. Copyright© 1973, 1978, 1984, 2011 by Biblica, Inc.™. Used by permission of Zondervan.

Scriptures marked (NKJV) are taken from the NEW KING JAMES VERSION (NKJV): Scripture taken from the NEW KING JAMES VERSION®. Copyright© 1982 by Thomas Nelson, Inc. Used by permission. All rights reserved.

Printed in the United States of America

This Handbook is dedicated to my wife, Dorothy, and to my four children: Tawana, Tara, Thomas IV, and Talia. I give special notice to each of my five grandchildren. I have come to realize that without my family enduring my madness and loving me despite my learning curve, I would not have grasped many of the life lessons that I have come to live by and I would not have learned the lessons that allow me to be so secure in my encouragement to you. Their love allows me to pass on to you the information found in this book.

For those of you who do not know me, you should know that I am blessed mightily by God to have the family that was given to me. Through good times and hard times, my family has traveled this journey with me, endured my mistakes, my bad choices, my short-comings and incidences of bad judgment, and yet, they continue to love me for me.

To them, I say, I am the one who has been given the greatest gift. I am so proud of each of you! So to each of you, all my love, my appreciation, and my heart.

Sincerely,
Thom, Baby, Dad, Pop, Poppi

The Colbert Family minus a grandson,
daughter-in-law, and grandson-in-law

One thing I realized while interacting and spending time with our youth is that virtually without fail, each of them would bend over backward to get the approval of their parents and/or significant adult in their lives.

Thomas "Uncle Thomas" Colbert
President, World Youth Ministries, Inc.

"Investing in Today's Youth…for a Brighter Tomorrow"
"Saving Future Generations by Connecting Families Today"

CONTENTS

Foreword...9

Chapter 1: On-the-Job Training...11

Chapter 2: The Numbers Tell Us a Story 18

Chapter 3: My Personal Gift to You—
Lessons I Learned in Life: Your Choices 20

Chapter 4: Lessons I Learned in Life: You and Others................27

Chapter 5: Lessons I Learned in Life: Your Leadership..............34

Chapter 6: A Few Additional Thoughts 43

Chapter 7: Keeping It Real..45

Chapter 8: Since Life Is a Teacher,
What Did We Really Learn? 48

FOREWORD

Children are our future. Our future is wrapped up inside of them. They are the promise that our families and our world will move forward.

Practically every civilized culture formulates guidelines to ensure family progression, but the ones that employ godly wisdom, biblical principles and persistent faith fare better than those that don't.

Our rapid technological changes that isolate individuals and fragment our families at an unprecedented pace demand that parents review and re-evaluate basic principles over and over again. Pastor Thomas Colbert, outstanding leader, teacher, and mentor of youth, employs a keen eye and a skillful hand in crafting an easy read and practical tool for all parents and those who truly care about producing families of high character.

Of course, no book in history qualified to speak on the subject of how to rear and train children more than the revelation of God, who renews, sustains, and creates life every day. I believe this work is inspired by God.

The Bible says that the parenting process is a complicated job, with eternal consequences. It behooves us all to get this right. No parent can afford to proceed without adequate preparation and know how. Pastor Thomas Colbert's excellent list of wisdom will serve to provide an armor of defense against all the wiles of the enemy. Therefore God has provided for us this timely "how to" direction for training a vulnerable generation. *A Handbook for Busy Parents* is a ready reference given in our time of need.

Bishop Horace E. Hockett,
Senior Pastor, Born Again Church and Christian Outreach Ministries
Presiding Bishop of the Kingdom Builders Network
Retired Educator

CHAPTER 1

On-the-Job Training

Parents will find themselves frequently at a point of despair, with feelings of failure, regretting years lost with their children and often wondering if they did enough. This is especially true with those who are called to the ministry. They wonder about their efforts in parenting as well as their duties in ministry. Under this mental duress, parents might find themselves questioning decisions that they made as they juggled ministry and family while just surviving life.

Through the ages, Satan has carried out his carefully planned attack upon the family. Just as a reminder to you that we have already been warned in scripture, "Now the serpent was more subtle than any beast of the field which the Lord God made" (Genesis 3:1a). Throughout the world that subtle troublemaker has carefully planted seeds of division and discord in families through a rising divorce rate, years of increasing abortions, growing divisions parent to child and spouse to spouse, as well as a constant diet of inappropriate behaviors by way of some television, movies, and genres of music. We see just overall bad human advice influenced by Satan himself.

The very foundation and strength in our churches, communities, and cities are undermined and as a result the traditional family is being formidably attacked from every direction. Separations, limited parenting skills, childcare problems, high debt, and low funds, insufficient maturity, and inadequate life skills are all factors impacting and lending to brokenness in the family.

We now live in a world gripped with a desire for constant hype and self-gratification. More than ever our youth show boredom and frustration and a sense of lost hope, often manifested through lack of attention to detail, short attention span, low motivation to accomplish, and a growing inability to form interpersonal, meaningful relationships. Victims of poor parenting, failing schools, and a lack of encouraging, motivating mentors in their lives, youth often feel powerless to have a voice or to make a difference.

Now while all of this is true, you, as a busy parent, must not believe that you are responsible! Yes, we must take responsibility that we indeed did contribute, at least partly, as a result of some of the bad choices we made but know this: this is not your fault. This attack is a spiritual matter, not of flesh and blood. It is the result of principalities, powers, rulers of darkness of this world, and wickedness in high places, all by the design of a subtle deceiver.

Remember these two things, my busy, new friend:

(1) You were required to learn by on the job training; and
(2) Your kids did not come with instructions!

Well, I've got good news for you! "All things" really do "work together for good to them that love God, to them who are called according to his purpose" (Romans 8:28 KJV).

Hallelujah! You're covered!

So, let me share with you a few of my hard-learned lessons. Let me be for you, a friendly guide as you go forward!

Things to Consider

1. Parents, you were not perfect either.

A scripture says, "Fathers, provoke not your children to wrath" (Ephesians 6:4 KJV), or "Fathers, do not exasperate your children; instead, bring them up in the training and instruction of the Lord (NIV).

Your sins of childish folly were not your undoing. In other words, they were not sins unto death. If you would just calm down, neither will your child's folly be his/her undoing. I know we want to raise them well and expect great things from our children, but expecting perfection of your children and constantly correcting them on every little thing changes correction to criticism. This will be one of the greatest areas of contention in the parent/child relationship. Ease up! You are not perfect! You are not God and your child knows it! God knows that you and your children are subject to sin and mistakes. That's why he sent Jesus.

Yes, you want your children to be good and successful, and you begin to think they must not make any mistakes but *give it a break!* When this attitude prevails, you will find yourself yelling about everything to the point that your words are no longer effective to correcting or even to influencing your children. Your presence will become a source of pain to them and while they might respect you and look your way while you are talking, know this, they are no longer listening!

2.   Let them make bad choices…sometimes.

This may sound like bad advice, but it is important that your child be allowed to say the wrong thing and/or make the wrong choice from time to time. For without it you would not learn how to be a good parent and the child would never realize the difference between right and wrong. As parents we must know that we too get it wrong sometimes, but we also must know the importance of "repenting" to the child, as well as to the Lord. You can be assured of this one thing, if your child is made to feel that he/she is the only one who must "*always*" be perfect or feels like the only one who ever makes the mistakes, that child will grow up broken, hesitant in decision-making, and ultimately a very frustrated adult.

3.   End the "preacher's kid" phenomenon.

The phenomenon of the "preacher's kid" came about mainly for two reasons:

a)   As mentioned above, the ministering parents will often try to run a mistake-free home and will find themselves in the posture of being unfair or intolerant regarding the child's natural learning process. They frequently find themselves unwilling to allow their child to have a choice in anything. Remember, by God's word, "the right of choice is in every man" (Deuteronomy 30:19–20) and the inability to exercise that right will result in rebellion. Now, because I hear you thinking out loud, let me say, I am not talking about you as a parent allowing your children to run wild and follow every whim of their young, inexperienced minds. See, you already know that to allow a child choice without loving direction would ruin the child and I repeat, "would ruin the child!"

Trust me; I had four chances to learn what I am now passing on to you for free. See, I do realize that in the culture of our day, there is an attack by "principalities, powers, and the rulers of darkness of this world" (Ephesians 6:12) against parents' right to rear their children. You should know as a parent, however, that you are justified and even encouraged to handle and address the selfishness and mischievous behaviors in your children's early years. In fact, the Bible teaches us about the "early years of folly found in our children" (Ecclesiastes 11:10). While I will always believe that children should be given opportunities to make basic choices, I am not totally devoid of the understanding that we as parents are called to train up our children in the way they should go (Proverbs 22:6). Just to help you, I'll add, training is forced obedience.

b) I do believe that the second reason for the "preacher's kid" phenomenon is that the minister's home *is* under even greater attack from the enemy, than non-ministry homes. There are greater incidences of attack from Satan and his imps, on both the parent and the child to get it wrong. This increased incidence of the satanic attack often causes the appearance of God's people being out of control, when in actuality, much of the pain and anger that we attribute to flesh and blood is caused by principalities, powers, and rulers of darkness of this world and that all is by the calculated attack of the old trickster, deceiver, the devil. Too often during this time of testing, many parents will fail to recognize these challenges as a time to show more love and support rather than anger and disgust. "For we wrestle not against flesh and blood, but against principalities, against powers, against the rulers of the darkness of this world, against spiritual wickedness in high places" (Ephesians 6:12).

4.   Make the right choice.

Remember, parent, life itself is a test and your job is to seek to make the right choices! The outcome of the choice is never your decision, but it is *always* the result of the choice that you made. God tells us, "I call heaven and earth to record this day against you, that I have set before you life and death, blessing and cursing: therefore, choose life, that both thou and thy seed may live" (Deuteronomy 30:19).

5.   Love them all the time

Love your children because of who they are, not because of what they do! Remember, *only God* can change a heart. Just do what you know to do and watch God be God.

6.   Seek balance.

To all parents, but especially to those who are ministers, there is a great need to learn balance in what is required for the work we are called to do for ministry and to that which is needed for the work we are called to do for family. When God called you, he knew you would have to be responsible to both tasks, so be confident of this: inside you are the abilities to do both and to do both well!

7. Trust God as you step.

Settle down and trust the steps as they are ordered by the Lord. The Bible declares, "The steps of a good man are ordered by the Lord: and he delighteth in his way" (Psalm 37:23).

8. Your time won't pause.

There is a biblical record of time standing still on one occasion. "And the sun stood still, and the moon stayed, until the people had avenged themselves upon their enemies… So, the sun stood still in the midst of heaven, and hasted not to go down about a whole day" (Joshua 10:13). Trust me that is not usually the case and you, my friends, are relegated to the normal twenty-four-hour day. Therefore, be sure to consciously think and arrange time for your children. Do not allow your ministry to take away from that family time. Now there will be times when you may have to cancel and reschedule, just don't forget the "reschedule" part. Remember, God knows your home duties and your work schedule. Without a doubt, he has provided time for both!

9. Grab the time.

Sometimes we need to be reminded to think through the little things, things such as remembering to show your kids that they really are your priority! Frequently as ministers of the gospel, and/or, just being active in the work of the church, we find ourselves out of town for days at a time, or otherwise unavailable for family. Your time away may be completely necessary, but remember, when you come in, let your family know that they are your priority. Take a moment to spend time with them, letting them know that you enjoy being with them and that you cherish every moment that you can spend with them, even with the demands posed by your calling in ministry or other job demands. It is important to make the time even if only for a moment to put your arm around them and give a peck on the cheek. Even small sincere gestures of affection will go a long way, where love is involved. Always recognize that your family, quite simply, is on loan to you for only a short amount of time.

I can attest to you from my own hard learned lessons that in time, you will realize that those little moments are precious and will go a long way in keeping fellowship and harmony within the family unit.

CHAPTER 2

The Numbers Tell Us a Story

I implore you, take a long and prayerful look at your priorities. Yes, *both* are important, but your family is your first ministry. Remember what I told you earlier: Inside you are the abilities to do both and to do both well.

Could this be your average day (see figures below)?

Work	eight hours
Travel to and from work	one and a half hours
Church Services/Activities	two hours
Daily Prayer and Study	two hours
Sleep	six hours
Leisure (chill) Time	one and a half hours
Interaction with church members and friends	two hours
Sub-total	twenty-three hours
Your Child	one hour

Just for thought, consider the gravity of the above figures.

Now consider this: Birth until legal age of eighteen years

Hours available for use	Time given to Child
Day = twenty-four hours	one hour
Week = 168 hours	seven hours
Month = 672 (thirty days per month)	28 hours (one day and four hours)

Year 365 days = 8,760 hours	365 hours (fifteen days of 365)
Eighteen Years = 6,570 days or 157,680 hours	6,570 hours (273-3/4 days)

As a faithful servant of the Lord, you will be, by necessity unavailable to be with your child for his/her one hour of the day. If you only spend an average of one hour per day with your child, consider this: of the 6,570 days of his/her life until age eighteen, and of the 157,680 available hours of eighteen years of your child's life, at one hour per day, with a schedule such as noted above, the ministry parent would only spend 273.75 days with that child! Wow! Who would have thought it?

Just being real. I've been there, done that.

Don't let numbers distress you. Knowledge is power and power can change circumstances!

It's never too late to reconnect.

CHAPTER 3

My Personal Gift to You— Lessons I Learned in Life: Your Choices

Over time I have learned many life lessons that I wish I had learned earlier. Now I know that for most of you I am not telling you anything that you don't already know, but the problem is that in our fast paced and often hectic schedules, we have let slip or have forgotten some of our most basic principles for survival and success. We forgot that we are helpers, one to another. If you find your brother in a fault, go to him in a way you would like to be approached. We forget to pray one for the other and we pass over other rules of caring.

Okay, some of you may not agree with me, but I hope, you will find a few jewels below that you can use and share with your children as they grow. Be encouraged as this is for certain: the longer you live and see them in action, the more you will realize, they heard and learned much more than you imagined! They will make you proud. So give your children a hand up. Give them information, knowledge of life lessons they can live by.

    1.   *Life presents us with challenges and obstacles, but it is our choice how we respond.*

We are faced with decisions daily. Some bring about good, some not so much good, and others even bring evil. See life is a choice and almost every thought of life comes as a choice, to be accepted or rejected. "Choose life so that you and your children may live" (Deuteronomy 30:19, NIV).

Yes, as much as we hate to admit it, we as parents are challenged to make right choices and assessments about everything we face in life. Many decisions must be made in a millisecond of thought and can set the very course of your life's destiny forever. That is why, for every man (hu-man), there must be a renewing of the mind (Romans 12: 2) and a fail-safe put in place. God is that fail-safe (Philippians 3:15) who will make clear to you how to off-set the damaging effects of self-fulfillment and desire (1 John 2:16), which infected man at the fall in the garden.

2. *Your choices influence your destiny.*

Without a doubt, life will bring upon each of us challenges and trials (Job 14:1). They will cover the gambit from the minor to the major and will influence the course of our lives. It is incumbent upon us, therefore, to develop a conscious thought process, so we will choose life and make right choices beneficial to ourselves, our families, and others. (Acts 27:18–44)

Let me share this story with you. This is a true story of a bright-eyed young man who, for the sake of this book, I will call Jesse. Jesse is a young man who began participating with our organization, World Youth Ministries (WYM). He was a middle school student. He could be described as a mischievous kid who loved basketball and hanging out with his friends. He was raised in an area plagued with high crime and other social ills. During his time with WYM, Jesse participated on the travel basketball team. As the youngest player on the team he learned important life skills, such as leadership, team-work, self-worth, and building healthy relationships. He served as an ambassador of WYM.

Although receiving guidance from WYM, Jesse was dealing with some behavioral issues at home and in school. The negative influences in his environment proved to be too strong and Jesse ended up getting into some trouble with the Department of Juvenile Justice, which earned him time in a secure facility. During this time of incarceration, he was able to reflect on the impact that WYM made in his life, which gave him the motivation needed to improve his life. Despite his situation at the time, he decided to choose life. Jesse began to focus on improving himself and, while incarcerated, earned his GED and HVAC certification, preparing him for jobs in heating, ventilation, and air conditioning.

Jesse is now a successful business owner in another state. He spends much of his time and resources "paying it forward." He frequently comes back home to give back to the community that helped shaped him. His main mission is to encourage youth that it is possible to change their lives no matter what mistakes they have made. His passion and life's testimony have created a platform for him to reach the masses, as he testified before a congressional committee as a living witness to this truth: *Troubled youth can turn their lives around with support and encouragement.* He uses social media to send the encouraging message on "People Can Change!" (#pplcanchange). While early challenges and some bad decisions on Jesse's part did set him on a path that could have caused him to give up, he found strength to choose life, to shape his destiny.

Now should he read my book, he will recognize himself. So to him I say, "Uncle Thomas is proud of you!"

3. *Your creator determines your purpose, but your choices determine your life.*

Contrary to popular thought, there is no such thing as "A Self-Made Man." Each of us has been formed by our Creator (Psalm 139:13–18) who expressly determined the purpose for our existence, and each has a God-given privilege of choice. Each of us has been taught throughout the course of life by our experiences and influences in the way we were raised, but none, not one of us, is a product of his own doing. Some of us are more freely blessed as a result of our choices and choices made by others that impact us. Life brings expected and unexpected circumstances, but how you react and what you do determine your destiny.

A few years ago I wrote a song, "Start All Over Again." Thank God, he allows us a re-do through his grace.

4. *Real choice occurs in the heart.*

Most of our life's situations are a direct result of decisions that we have made and many of those decisions were, no doubt, fueled by our own selfish desires and thoughts. Too often we find ourselves in a pickle, because of the inner counsel given to us by ourselves. We decide based on our own feelings. It would be wise to remember that the self can give you ungodly counsel (Psalm 1:1). Pastor T.D. Jakes said it well in one of his messages, "The enemy is in me!" Remember this, my friend, true godly and positive change in our lives can never occur, until we become willing to accept godly counsel and become willing to accept responsibility (good or bad) for decisions that were of our own choosing.

5. *You are not a victim of circumstances.*

In one of his sermons, Pastor John Hagee said, "You are not the victim of your circumstance; you are the victim of your choices." This is so true. So often in our lives we try to pass the blame for our circumstances onto others, blaming them for their actions. Some of us never learn that our circumstances might be, in part, the result of a connected or relevant event caused by others, but primarily the outcome is the result of our choices.

6. *Just because life happens to you, does not mean you cannot have life for you.*

Just so you know, "Life happens" (Job 14:1–2). Now let me let you off the hook because I do realize that life can give us much justification to complain. Yes, I do acknowledge that life can bring you many obstacles, trials, and many of us have felt the pains of being challenged by those who will persecute and revile us unfairly.

Years ago, we had a young girl come to the city to travel with us on one of our summer tours. I began interacting with this young girl and found that she loved singing. While she was shy and appeared to be holding back, our choir directress (who is quite amazing herself) saw something in this young girl and asked that she would lead one of the songs while on the tour. *Wow*! This young girl blossomed and really shined! Well some may say, "Okay, she could sing," but what you don't know is how this young girl could have allowed her life situation to break her and stop her from seeking to have a life. See, this youngster had witnessed her mother and father being killed as an intruder broke into their home. She was spared as her dad pushed her into a closet, to hide her out of harm's way.

When life happens as it always will, choose life and live.

7.   *Others can give you the tools, but success in life will come by your choice.*

Two men in a dry land are given shovels to dig a well. One immediately goes to work digging until he strikes a deep-water stream and now has water for his family and him. The other just sat around contemplating all the work involved and what it would be like if he did all that digging and found no water. Oh well, think about it. What would you choose to do?

8.   *The difference between a realist, a pessimist, and an idealist is perspective.*

A realist sees what is.
A pessimist sees what might happen.
An idealist sees a world of possibility.

9.   *The beauty of a dreamer is that he sees what can be.*

Too often, we are held back from great accomplishment and heroic feats (1 Samuel 17:26) because we allow ourselves to be tied to what is, and to the history of how it has always been. Instead, we need to learn and believe so we can see the substance of a thing before it is manifested (Hebrews 11:1).

10. *The awesome thing about wisdom is that it knows what is, but always encourages what can be.*

While we all need someone to speak into our lives, we must develop in ourselves the wisdom to seek wise counsel (Proverbs 11:14). We must realize that not every voice should be allowed the right to speak into us (Psalm 1:1–2, Galatians 1:8–10). Now let's be warned against allowing the habit of "stinking thinking" to become prevalent in our lives as a result of bad advice from others or from our own lack of wisdom.

11. *Learn who you are and move in the confidence of who you are.*

We all have in us, the potential to overcome all the obstacles and trials that come against us, but you must learn to trust that the Creator who filled you with purpose is prepared to fight on your behalf. (2 Kings 6:15–18). You must ask, believing that he will answer (Matthew 21:22).

Let me say here, I have been blessed to witness positive change in the lives of many youth, but unfortunately, too often, I have also seen those who struggled because they thought they had no one who believed in them. See I was not kidding when I said each of them would bend over backward to get the approval of their parents and/or other significant adults in their lives. Yes, we must teach our children and even correct them when they are wrong, but this must be tempered with our desire for their good (Ephesians 6:4).

As the result of parents' busy schedules, too often children are being left to interact with the always available, destructive influences of too much social media, Internet, and the most subtle sneaky one, television. If we take time to look deeper, we can see many shows, even kids programming, are pushing a very destructive, perverse, and pervasive agenda.

Now I do wish right here that I could give you a pass because, yes, the schedules of some busy parents can become hectic and may even feel overwhelming. Even so, as parents we must always be watchful and prayerful; remember, *you* are the strong man of the house and without your watchful eye, your child can be snatched away (Luke 11:21). Our children are our most valued possession and are worth fighting for.

CHAPTER 4

Lessons I Learned in Life: You and Others

Very early in life our children begin trying to understand themselves and how to deal with others. Most of what they learn will come from watching us.

12. *Purpose is like a fingerprint: it's specific to you alone.*

Two of the greatest lessons you can ever teach your child are that each of us is unique and that we all are created with purpose. The greatest honor we can ever give to our creator is to fulfill his plan for our lives, according to his purpose for us. See, an expensive knife might be turned around and its handle used to bang a nail into the wall. It can be damaged in the process because that knife falls short of fulfilling its purpose until it does what the cutler created it to do.

13. *Time trying to be like someone else is time wasted.*

Too often people miss knowing the greatness of who they are, while trying so diligently to be like someone else. They don't recognize their own value and miss attaining the beauty and power of who they could become. (Ephesians 4:1–7). Know this, we each have our place, and if we are not careful, one can be damaged trying to be someone else, doing something we were not created to do.

14. *Each of us was created by God with the ability for greatness.*

Inside of us is everything we need to accomplish that which we were created to be and to do. The problem is too many people look at the success of others who are walking in their calling and try to become that other person, instead of seeking the will of the Lord for their own lives, and learning to walk in the vocation wherewith they are called.

For years, I have been blessed to work with young people along with a lot of great parents and volunteers. Some of the young people have phenomenal voices. One of the biggest problems I found to releasing them to become their most powerful self, using their voices with true passion, was to convince them to seek to develop their own style. I'd tell them to stop trying so much to sing a song just like the recording artist that they were trying to imitate.

Please keep at the forefront of your mind, children can be like sponges. For the most part they will take on habits, attitudes and personalities like those that they witness and learn from while in the household with their parents.

15. *Be an encourager and find those who encourage you.*

Years ago, I was privileged to work with five of the most talented young girls that I have ever had the opportunity to work with during my years of ministry. I kid you not, there was something extraordinary about the sound of these five young girls as their voices blended. They had a sound that was as good, or better than most of the professional groups of the time. My intent was to form a smaller group with these girls because it would be less costly and easier to move than our ministry's over 150-member Community Gospel Choir.

Three of these girls were relatively confident in their abilities to sing. Two acted with less confidence when singing without the choir. One of the two would always stand a foot or two behind the others when singing. She was a brilliant student taking accelerated classes throughout high school, but when it came to her singing, she would always shy away.

The other of the two had one of the most beautiful voices around. She enjoyed singing but would have to be made to sing. Even then we would have to give her a microphone just to hear her part when all the others were singing. When talking and kidding with the others she was no wallflower; she was funny. Yet when it came to her singing she only did so with much encouragement (and/ or an occasional threat).

She struggled in her schoolwork and was doing a good job making herself believe that she was not a good student. She constantly made remarks about how bad a student she was, convincing herself that academics was not her thing. This attitude was eroding her confidence, causing her to unduly struggle with high school.

Trust me, each one of the five had her own set of challenges and woes, but this is not the end of the story. I just talked about two of the five girls, to help me land on this point. As great a sound as these girls had when they all came together, the one thing they had that was even greater than their sound, was that they encouraged each other to keep going. They never allowed one of the others to give up. They spoke life into each other, until they could begin to believe in themselves.

See, that is why it is so important that we too speak life into our own children. No matter their confidence level or even their level of ability (or lack of) they need us to be like these five girls. Love enough to not allow your children to accept defeat but keep encouraging them until it becomes a part of them and they themselves can see success within themselves.

Now of the two girls in the example, one has graduated college, with a degree in accounting. The other one, who could not see herself ever doing well in school, went on to college, did so well that she was on the college's Presidential Scholar List for Excellence in Academics and now has a degree in social work and will graduate soon with a master's degree. As to her singing, she has blossomed so much so that she can carry a whole section if need be. Of the other three, one is a doctor in physical therapy, another is a registered nurse, and the third has a degree in business marketing management.

16. *We are no better than any others, but we are a step ahead by the grace of God.*

I know you have seen people who, no matter the conversation, they are an authority. They always try to one-up you and give you advice, even on things in which you are the one with the expertise. Now you may be strong and confident in who you are, but in my years of observing people, especially youth, I have found that there are personalities who will bow down to that authoritative one, and if they are not careful, they can lose themselves, their identities, and begin to deny or forget their own self-worth. This has become quite evident to me in my over forty years of ministry dealing with both adults and youth alike. This syndrome will manifest in all age groups. I have also recognized, however, that when an individual is encouraged and reminded that each one was created with purpose, when affirmed, that one tends to awaken and come alive, beginning to bring ideas to the table.

The Bible declares in the book of Proverbs, there is value found in the multitude of counsel (Proverbs 11:14–15, Proverbs 24:6). Overbearing personalities who will cut off and deny other opinions, however, can be a very destructive force in the workplace, in government, and also in the family. Too often great talent and good ideas are squashed as some are swept aside and consistently denied opportunity to express themselves.

During my childhood, I found myself in that very situation often, feeling that others were more important than I and that my opinion did not matter. I remember vividly, the conscious feeling of needing to become very protective of my siblings that they should never have to be made to feel that type of pain. Oh yes, even now I can remember the feelings of loneliness and rejection.

Whew, enough down that rabbit hole of despair, because the good news is, I was one of the blessed ones. I had someone speak into my young life and help me understand that no matter where destiny may take you, destiny can never change your purpose, for purpose is determined by the creator of a thing. That reminded me that I was created by God and that I was created for good works

(Ephesians 2:10). From there, I learned to become confident in who I am and to stop competing with people on their turf. Even when in their territory, I learned to seek to be the best me, rather than trying to beat them.

Wow! Once I got that, a light came on and my self-confidence began to grow. The ugly faces that I had envisioned around me, the frowns and scowls on faces began to change and I could see smiles.

Learning these lessons taught me that I never want anyone to feel the pain I felt, no matter who they are. No matter their pedigree or no degree, I want them to be thankful for who they are created to be, for *no one* can be a better you than you can be!

17. *A dreamer's poison is someone who constantly reminds him of what is.*

We must be careful as we navigate through life, to learn to properly assess information spoken into our spirit, for it can move us from a place of victory and hope as overcomers, to one of fear and defeat. (1 Kings 19:2–4). Learn to hear and adjust if need be, but always walk in the Spirit, knowing in whom you trust.

18. *Sometimes you must give something for nothing.*

Keeping your hands clinched only on what you have in your hands can prevent you from embracing something you really want.

19. *The key to restoration and healing lies in the heart of the offended.*

The heart of an offended fool fails to recognize the opportunity to forgive.

Forgive quickly when you are offended, for it frees you to move on. Holding a grudge will forever keep you at the point of where the offence occurred.

20. *Decide who has the right to criticize you.*

Any person who cannot encourage and honor the right and good that you do is disqualified from the right to criticize your shortcomings.

Nuff said!

You just remember and know this about your haters: they usually hate because your light is shining brightly in their faces.

21. *If someone can take away your ability to choose, you never had it anyway.*

Now, this one can be a hard one to recognize, and in most cases it will be because of your own ego. We like to feel important, or at least feel that our opinion matters.

Never allow yourself to be dumped on by people who do not have your best interest at heart. Their actions will prove over and over that they only protect their interest and could care less about you or your family, and whether your children will have Christmas or not. Don't be fooled. If they place you in a position of power, but never allow you to actually use that power, then don't allow your ego to blind you. Wake up and smell the coffee! You may have the position, but you never had the power.

22. *Take on your responsibilities and your blame.*

Learn this now, the stress of taking on the responsibility for your own actions and allowing yourself to take on the blame of others carries implications for what your children may learn, as they observe. That affects their decision-making and how they relate to others throughout their lifetimes.

23. *Not everyone who boards your bus is interested in your destination.*

24. *Life is for learning.*

Let me help you gain another perspective. You see, all along you thought life was just sticking it to you. It was. Life is "full of troubles," but when you add in the "God factor" and his love for you, now, you see what had happened. Life was not making you lose, but making you learn.

25. *Be sure that you are one of your best friends.*

Often men and women fail in their ability to show real godly love, because they are conflicted with their thoughts about what they want, in contrast to what they have (Matthew 6:25–30). We must all seek and learn to be content (Hebrews 13:5 and Philippians 4:11–13). Oh yes, I can hear you in the Spirit, beating yourself, as you remember all the missed opportunities of your past. Well, now that you are more acquainted with me and know that I mean you no harm, please accept this word of encouragement as I take this opportunity to speak into your Spirit. "Get over it!" Stop beating yourself. We have all missed opportunities of our past. We have all at one time or another fallen short of the glory of God for our life's purpose (Romans 3:23), so now my friend, all is not lost. Be your best friend. See how you gained wisdom as you experienced your past and the grace of God still now has your committed and thankful heart, open and ready to receive from him, a greater anointing to serve and power to get wealth.

CHAPTER 5

Lessons I Learned in Life: Your Leadership

At home, at work, in the community, at school, in ministry, and wherever you are, you are a leader. What do you do with that calling and what do children learn from your lead?

26. *You are a leader and therefore, a standard of strength to those who follow you.*

Often circumstances of life can cause you to feel that you are all but defeated. You feel like you've tied a knot in the rope of life and you're barely holding on. Yes, life gets challenging, but the key here is you are still holding on. You have not given up.

The story of Gideon, found in Judges 6:11–17, tells of a man pitying himself as he was surrounded by obstacles. The Lord was with him and brought him victory. God will be your strength. Yes, times will get hard and you will feel pushed to your very limit, but know this, those who belong to the Lord and will submit to his power, rather than their own strength, will overcome. If you would leave your pity party, your fear and doubt, and believe, you will raise a standard for others to follow. Learn to let the confidence of the Lord rule in your spirit (Psalm 24:7–10) and know, with God all things are possible.

27. *Learn to walk tall with your head up. It is your time. Do not waste it.*

Learn to think well about who you are, for until you can embrace who you are, it is difficult to move forward with the passion needed to fire your engine for success. Teach your children to do the same.

I learned this painful lesson: If we are not careful, we really can create issues that can be a challenge for our young children. While we should not give our children (or any other child) a free pass to be substandard in what they do, we can and should make a greater effort to focus and allow their gifts and talents to shine. I was just slow y'all, so please let me encourage you. Learn this lesson before you run the risk of crushing your child's desire to try.

Case in point, my only begotten son, in his younger years demonstrated great ability to sing with an extraordinarily strong voice. He was determined that his tenor section would not be second to any other section. As a child he could sing as well as, and with the strength and quality, of a well-known artist. If I called that artist's name you would immediately know who I was talking about.

I remember going to my son one day and asking him to lead a song by the artist. I immediately saw the hesitancy in my son. I took it as his unwillingness to try, but the words out of his mouth when I challenged him floored me. He explained that if he led the song, he thought people would say the only reason he was allowed to lead the song was because he was my son. That is when it hit me. I had not allowed my son the option of feeling confident in his own abilities. I loved singing and did so in many arenas. Truth be told, my son could sing me under a table, but because of an atmosphere that I had established, he was not confident in and able to see the magnificence of his own gift.

Now, I am glad to say that after working through that situation, my son became one of the leading vocalists in our choir. Today he has grown up and very rarely sings but that is by his own choice and not because of my shadow. He treads his own path and now casts his own shadow. He works in mid-management with a major corporation and finds time to give back by serving on the Board of Directors of our WYM Ministry. He's helping his Pops to stay focused as we continue together our vision of "investing in today's youth, for a brighter tomorrow."

Life's not too shabby when the light comes on, and you learn to walk tall. Hold your head up. Recognize your time. And do not waste it.

28. *Stand for excellence.*

Now let me come clean here for the purpose of full disclosure. Yes, I pray these are great lessons for parents to teach their children early in life, however, truth be told, I did not "get it" for much of what I can now speak and write about until later in my life. Much of it I had to learn on the fly while raising my children, who BTW (by the way), helped me to grow up and taught me a few things, too. Allow me to qualify my point and give you pause for thought, first by saying that no parent should have to *lower their standards for excellence* or feel the need to *dumb down* their quest, just for the sake of making their children feel better about themselves. Stop playing a game and letting them win all the time just to make them feel good. Doing so can make them weak and can give them a false sense of security about who they are. It can become a set-up for failure when real life comes upon them and they are forced to perform.

Check yourself, though, and know that you're showing excellence in your own actions. Show that excellence is really your standard.

29. *Learn to speak well of yourself.*

Your subconscious self will form the conscious responses for your life based on every word and interaction in your life. Your thoughts are the foundation for who you ultimately become (Proverbs 23:7), and of what you choose to believe. What you believe will rule the choices that you will make for your life and, therefore, will also affect those who are around you and those for whom you are responsible.

Too often our subconscious is influenced by negative thoughts or words said to us.

I have been the victim of my own "stinking thinking." Years ago while in college my life was on quite a different trajectory. I was preparing to go into medical school, but I was told by a well-meaning counselor that I would not be able to work while in medical school. I was immediately taken back to some of my feelings of insufficiency felt in my childhood. With that defeated thinking being allowed back into my thought processes, I let go of what had been a lifelong dream, and that decision drastically changed the focus of my life.

Thank God, that is not the end of the story. He had a purpose and a plan for my life (Ephesians 2:10). I do thank God for his grace and mercies that cause all things to work together for good for I was called with a desire to fulfill what he placed in me to accomplish on this earth (Romans 8:28). So, let me pose this question to you: Who will you allow to use words and destroy your dream? By now you must know that that was a trick question for the only one who can really destroy your dream is you. Choose to believe in yourself and speak well of yourself. Yes, life will give you lemons, just make lemonade, and hold on to your God-given dreams!

30. *Always speak truth, but do so cautiously.*

The right words, spoken out of time can cause irrefutable damage to the spirit of a man often never to be undone (Ecclesiastes 3:1–8). Never be afraid to speak the truth, but always use caution as to when to speak it. Unless the time is right, some things are better left unspoken, even if they are true (Proverbs 12:17–22).

31. *It is better to deal with the consequences of truth than to lower your morals to the compromise of a lie.*

Early in life, I learned that lying was not worth the expended energy needed to keep up with the lie. I could not keep up. I do not know how, but my mom and dad seemed to instinctively know when I was lying and Thomas and Myrtis Colbert believed in paying you "the wages" of lying. Thank God for my parents! Even while making me serve out the punishment for my dishonesty, they would treat me with all the loving kindness of being their son.

Case in point, I only remember stealing once in my life. One day I had walked to the store with my cousin. We took our bottles to return for deposit so that we could buy ourselves a treat. Yes, we were able to do that back in the day. That day I wanted more than the deposit from my bottles would buy. So I got my treats, took them to the counter and paid for them with my newly-earned bottle deposit. I hid a candy bar, however, because I wanted it but did not have enough money to purchase it from my returned bottles that day. After making my purchase I left, yes, feeling guilty, yet exhilarated that I had my candy bar, and *no one* was any the wiser. Boy, was I ever going to enjoy that gooey chocolate, caramel, and peanuts!

Now you would have to know parents of my mom and dad's era. Parents watched and cared enough to get into the "who, what, where, when, and why" of their children's business. They made it their business while taking on the responsibility of how their children turned out in life. So wouldn't you know it, my dad saw me eating my candy bar and wanted to know where I had gotten it. I began to explain that I had paid for it using the deposit money from my bottles, but immediately he responded, "You did not have that many bottles with you."

Well, he takes it upon himself to take me back to the store (mind you, I had to walk to get there the first time), call the store owner to the front and then tells the man, "My son, has something he wants to tell you." What! No, I did not have something I wanted to tell. Our coming back to the store was all his idea. Oh well, I had to come clean and admit that I had stolen the candy bar.

After my confession, my dad, and the store owner arranged that I would work at the store to pay for having stolen from the store. After this my dad takes me home and deals with the situation (you know what I mean) to be sure that I remembered who I am and the value of being honest. Then he tells my mom. While the punishment stood neither of them ever mentioned the situation to me again.

Now this, for me, was rubbing salt in my wound. Here I was being untruthful and *what*? They punish me for the lie, but otherwise act as if nothing is wrong. So now I have a dilemma. I have lied, I know that they know that I lied, and now I know they are disappointed in me, but they are not bothering me over and over about my sin and wrongdoing. I learned a valuable lesson that day!

That being said please let me not paint myself as if in a white robe with a halo. Since that time I have committed much sin and have told many lies in my weakness as man, but in my heart I know these things are not and should not be my practice. I now realize that when I do these things, I have sinned and remain in *need* of a Savior. Thank God that in my guilty, fallen, and "unable to keep myself" life, I have that Savior and advocate in Jesus Christ, who bears my sin and pleads my case before the God of justice. See I have tried being perfect, but it has never worked. The most that the testimony of my life alone could earn me is still a penalty of death. So in my heart I deal daily with the consequence of the truth that "without Christ, I am a sinner," and therefore, must never lower myself to the compromise of living the lie that I have not fallen. While we may fall, in Christ we are forgiven.

32. *Vision does not require visual sight, just faith determined to accomplish it.*

If you can see it and believe it, you can accomplish it (Hebrew 11:1).

33. *Do not allow the word "can't" to become part of your regular vocabulary.*

If you have to use the word, use it cautiously and sparingly. The most damaging critic of a person comes from inside the mind of the one who has no personal confidence and has not found the ability to trust God.

I am accused of making all the kids who were a part of the WYM Community Gospel Choir think that they could sing. I realized that not all would lead songs while we were on our tour, but our philosophy is that failure to try will lead to hesitancy and self-doubt in seeking to accomplish in other areas of life. With God, all things are possible (Mark 10:27).

34. *Accept second if you must, but do not ever settle for it.*

I know that many would possibly disagree with this statement on its surface but go with me for a moment. This lesson is not about being prideful, but about developing within a desire for excellence with a "never give up" attitude.

35. *Slippin' and dippin' ain't nothing but trippin'.*

The integrity of the upright guides them, but the unfaithful are destroyed by their duplicity (Proverbs 11:3 NIV).

Approximately thirty years ago, I received a phone call from one of the choir members, a fourteen-year-old girl, who wanted to talk. Now I thought she would be telling me about boy/girl relationship problems, so I rehearsed in my head different scenarios of which I might be asked to respond. To my surprise, when the young girl began to speak, she also began to cry. She told me of how she no longer wanted to sell drugs. By allowing her to speak, I learned that this fourteen-year-old girl had been recruited to sell drugs at her school. In doing so, she also was taking two handguns to school. I talked with her and encouraged her by telling her that from that day on she would never have to sell the drugs again. The situation was handled. I then asked her, "Why the two handguns?" Her young, fourteen-year-old mind told me, "Cause if I get caught with one, I would still have the other one." She didn't realize that if she was caught with even one gun, that she would be expelled from school. I asked and she surrendered both guns to me.

I am so very glad that this young girl felt she could trust me and decided to talk with me, but how many others, don't have anyone that they feel they can talk to, and they keep slippin' and dippin', thinking that they are getting away, but all they are doing is trippin'.

As the adage goes, "That done in the dark, will come to the light" (Ecclesiastes 12:14).

36. *Your reputation is golden.*

Treat it that way. Proverbs 22:1 says a good name is better than wealth.

Opportunity will come knocking on the door to those who show promise, but for the rest, they must dig and search for it.

37. *Until you know who you are, you will not know how to become what you wish to be.*

Most parents fall into the self-made trap of wishing so much for their children's future that they fail to look in or to even ask the child what they want to become. This almost always results in conflict. Yes, parents can be a great resource and help to their children in navigating and plotting each child's life path. You will always be a resource for your children, but be warned, *do not* get in the habit of making decisions "for" your children as they grow more into their young adult lives. A child who is not allowed to make some decisions will grow up to be, in many cases, a very insecure adult and very hesitant to make decisions quickly. This ultimately will lead to your children becoming frustrated. It will, most likely, be a frustrating factor to their mate in life.

Teaching and encouraging your children, as you engender in them the confidence to try, allowing them to try, fail, and try again, will help them learn early, their likes and dislikes, their strengths and weaknesses too, as they begin to realize who they are and what they wish to become in life.

38. *Serve well, lead well.*

While people will frequently follow a dynamic personality, their passion to follow wanes, as they fail to feel any concerns for their own well-being or for their needs coming from their leader. The greatest way there is to endear yourself in the hearts of people so that they love you as they follow you is to show them by your actions, your concern, and care for their needs.

39. *The greater your ability to serve, the greater your ability to lead.*

Too often we are led by the brokenness of selfishness, that nagging attribute which came with the fall of man. Sin has dug into man's pride and caused men to work against each other, never wanting to be "one-upped" by the other. This subtle deceit frequently causes men to waste valuable resources that each could bring to the table. Instead they spend time fighting each other rather than fighting the common enemy. That is why we must be watchful and prayerful about what drives us (1 John 2:15–17). With self out of the way, we can better find avenues to the greater good. Think about this. While it is true that the leader is needed, it is those who serve, who actually get the work done. As you serve, the greater is your ability to lead and the deeper your conviction to service.

40. *A life worth living is a life worth living well.*

Over the years, I have learned that life brings two things: (1) the opportunity for success (life), or (2) the opportunity for failure (death). Too often we allow ourselves to believe or to equate our life's worth with the abundance of toys and comforts that we have in our possession. Too often that skewed perception is passed on to our children. Jesus teaches us that it is not about how much you have (Luke 12:15). You just learn to seek God and his righteousness (Matthew 6:33) and let him take care of the rest (Jeremiah 29:11).

CHAPTER 6

A Few Additional Thoughts

- After being away all day or for extended periods of time, do not come in on the phone and use up the time you could spend with your child.
- If you are willing to make time and talk with others when you are tired, then be willing to make time for your children too. Suck it up and know you are equipped!
- Spending time with your friends is good for your emotional health, just do not forget, spending time with your child is good for your geriatric years. That child may have to take care of you one day.
- There must be order. You must be: (1) the parent to train, (2) a friend to listen and discuss, and (3) the judge and disciplinarian when needed.
- Tread wisely. The teacher is not always right. Remember there are two sides to every conflict.
- Again, tread wisely. Your child is not always right. Remember there are two sides to every conflict.
- Children need healthy food for proper nutrition, growth, and strength. Unfortunately, in many cases, healthy food is not convenient. You must make the time! Repeat after me, *"My child 'is' my priority!"*
- Yes, you love your child, but without taking time for yourself, you can never consistently show your child real love. Too much self-sacrifice gives the child a false view of life and can lead to the child becoming selfish and unrelent-

ing in demands on your time, energy, and, of course, your money.

- Lastly, decompress! Your job is not to determine the outcome, but to be honest and always do your best. Make sure that when the dust settles you are still on the Lord's side.

CHAPTER 7

Keeping It Real

In the scriptures, there is a statement of caring that is used by the apostle Paul that I wish to adopt as I very carefully tip-toe through my discussion here with you.

Nobody told me how painful ministry would be, neither did they tell me that living life, trying to be faithful, honorable and true to God would bring out every one of the big dogs of hell on my tracks.

In order to be an encouragement to you let me say this: you may wrestle with thoughts of failure, doubts, and insufficiency. Those might be thoughts you have had, are having, or will have. As you look back over the story of your life you'll find yourself grading your past actions and past choices that you made or failed to make. Let me, in the best way I can think of at this moment, say to you: *stop it*! That die is already cast and truthfully, there is nothing that you can do to change any of it, except to maybe make an apology here or there, but even that would not change the past.

Now it pains me to have to admit it so publicly, but in the spirit of being truthful and as transparent as possible, let me say this. During my journey, I have made some drastic, bone-head choices and mistakes. Some brought much pain to my family, and if the truth be told, to my reputation and my financial status. Bad choices just negatively impacted greatly the things that I have been able to accomplish in my life. That is life, however, and life goes on and does not ask your permission.

I have made choices, and I know some of you have also, and done things that we thought were the right thing at the time, but later realized that we had made yet another daft decision. Now, I do not know about you but over the years, I have done so on many occasions. So let me encourage you, if I may. Part of why this book is so important to me is to write to you. Life is not easy. We are warned, "Man that is born of a woman is of a few days, and full of trouble" (Job 14:1). It is what it is and whatever was dished up to you is what you got. Now you can either let it poison you or you can let it nourish you for, once again, the choice is yours.

This time allow me to speak into your spirit as you consider your choices. Just think about it for a moment. You cannot change your past. You did the best you could, with the "time, talent, and treasures" you had as Dr. Tony Evans would say. Backward is never the safe way to look if you intend to go forward. So be encouraged. It is God who judges your missteps, your bad decisions as you tried to do the right thing in your attempts to be faithful, to balance commitment to calling and commitment to family. God judges, not by what you did, but by what was the intent of your heart when you made the choice you made.

> But the Lord said unto Samuel, Look not on his countenance, or on the height of his stature; because I have refused him: for the Lord seeth not as man seeth; for man looketh on the outward appearance, but the Lord looketh on the heart. (1 Samuel 17:7)

So, Hallelujah! The Lord's grace and mercy have got you covered. Repent for your bad choices and know that your failures are covered by the blood of a risen Savior, who forgives and brings to you lively hope, that life is not over. You are allowed to learn from your past and now choose life.

> I call heaven and earth as witnesses today against you, that I have set before you life and death, blessing and cursing; therefore choose life, that both you and your descendants may live; that you

may love the Lord your God, that you may obey His voice, and that you may cling to him, for he is your life and the length of your days; and that you may dwell in the land which the Lord swore to your fathers, to Abraham, Isaac, and Jacob, to give them. (Deuteronomy 30:19–20, NKJV)

CHAPTER 8

Since Life Is a Teacher, What Did We Really Learn?

Well, my friend, as we end our journey together with this chapter let us consider what things we have learned. Yes, we! I, too, had things to learn. You see if I learned anything along this journey it is that my life story goes far deeper than myself and far beyond myself, just as your story goes beyond you. Our stories are what we know and how we learned that which we know. I have come to realize that each story is actually a guide to teach others how to navigate through all the muddle we face in our lives. Our stories give each and every one of us the chance to make the right choice and to choose for ourselves this thing called "life."

So, what then is "life" and why is it so important that we should choose it? If we go to the dictionary for our definition, we find that life is "the condition that distinguishes animals and plants from inorganic matter, including the capacity for growth, reproduction, functional activity, and continual change preceding death."

Now, that definition, I suppose, would be fine for one who has no hope for greater or for one who believes that life only consists of that which precedes death. But wow! Is that all there is to life, that which happens while we have a heartbeat and breath in our bodies, or is there something else that must be considered? What about those of us who believe that there is more, that life continues beyond the funeral? "He that hath the Son hath life; and he that hath not the Son of God hath not life" (1 John 5:12). If this viewpoint be true, then there is much to be considered. One would plan for life seeing that without having the Son of God the only opportunity is for death, not life.

We recognize that we are all individuals and that we each look at things differently, considering our experiences and our vantage point in life. That includes those of us who have been presented with the task of raising children who did not come with the instructions stamped on their back. Let us settle in and think. Life is too short to suffer needlessly worrying about our past, about our everyday and future decisions as we learn to navigate this path of life. BTW, I am not talking about times when you choose to bury your head and don't try to do what you could do, when you should suck it up and do something.

My story then speaks to our assurance, that no matter what our vantage point, no matter our experiences of life, there is a hero. The beauty is the heart of the hero, Jesus, who brings to each of us every opportunity to believe and choose the life of our future. So, my friends, choose life, that you and your children may live!

Now to the millions who will read this book (hey a fella can hope, can't he?), I have not ever ventured to take on the task of writing a book before. That task in my mind was way out of my comfort zone. I have noticed, however, that over the years, my views about my purpose began to become clearer and more focused. I do not ever wish to be so presumptuous as to write a book telling others what they should or should not do, but I have written this to share what I have learned in hopes of helping you.

Remember this, if you don't know anyone else who is, know that I am praying for you.

Sincerely,
Uncle Thomas

ABOUT THE AUTHOR

Thomas "Uncle Thomas" Colbert

In approximately 1975, while a young minister and fresh out of college, Thomas E. Colbert III served under the direction of his then pastor, Supt. Owen Smith. He became greatly concerned with the direction and the declining respect for authority of the youth in his community. With the encouragement of his pastor to pray and follow as the Lord would lead, young Colbert began pulling groups of young people together to show them new focus and direction, to develop acceptable social skills and citizenship habits.

With increasing positive response from many of the youth in the community, Colbert believed the Lord was giving him an even greater urge within, to continue working with various groups and in settings of youth within the community. More and more, Colbert began interacting with growing numbers of youth. Subsequently, youth of all ages began coming to him expressing their desire to be a part and to join in with the activities whenever he planned them. He began noticing that, as a whole, many of the youth whom he met and interacted with maintained a desire to do well. Virtually all of them had a hope for approval from parents and adult leaders. With this revelation he began to pray for direction, to assure that no youth would develop an attitude of uselessness, fear, or doubt about their ability to succeed in the future. As time passed and prayer continued, the vision began to come into greater focus, not without great challenges, of course.

Following the death of his spiritual mentor, Supt. Smith, Colbert continued pursuing his calling though now under his new pastor, Elder J.L. Brown and eventually Pastor E.L. Sheppard. The vision continued and began to come more and more into focus and in 1984, World Youth Ministries was incorporated with the State of Florida as a not-for-profit organization, with a vision of "investing in today's youth...for a brighter tomorrow."

World Youth Ministries

On August 18, 1995, the Internal Revenue Service awarded WYM a 501(c)(3) status. Since that time, WYM has touched thousands of youth.

As a part of its vision, WYM will plan and incorporate WYM member chapters and/or partners with other like-minded organizations. These must be in communities where opportunity for growth is evident to the organization and/or where grassroots supporters for our mission and vision make formal application to develop a chartered chapter in the organization via our WYM website (http://worldyouthministries.org).

For those who are genuinely interested in being a force to make a difference in the lives of youth and families in your community, reach out to us via our website to join our WYM family. Leave your contact information and someone will respond.

All applications will be considered by our Chapter Selection Committee and must be approved by the WYM Board of Directors. All applicants selected, *must* pass a background check prior to the final review for selection by the WYM President and Board of Directors.

See us: WYM website http://worldyouthministries.org
Like us: http://www.facebook.com/wyminc

CPSIA information can be obtained
at www.ICGtesting.com
Printed in the USA
BVHW061329020321
601496BV00012B/1746